MW00423711

GOLDEN BEAUTY BOSS

THE STORY OF
MADAME SARA SPENCER
WASHINGTON
AND THE APEX EMPIRE

**CHERYL WOODRUFF BROOKS,
M.B.A., M.A.**

SUNBURY PRESS

Mechanicsburg, PA USA

Published by Sunbury Press, Inc.
Mechanicsburg, Pennsylvania

www.sunburypress.com

ISBN: 978-1-62006-261-6 (Trade paperback)

Library of Congress Control Number: 2020932598

FIRST SUNBURY PRESS EDITION: February 2020

Product of the United States of America
0 1 1 2 3 5 8 13 21 34 55

Set in Adobe Garamond
Designed by Crystal Devine
Cover by Lawrence Knorr
Edited by Erika Hodges and Lawrence Knorr

Continue the Enlightenment!

This book is dedicated to
Madame Sara Spencer Washington.
Thank you for your courageous vision.

This book is also dedicated to every woman in
the world in pursuit of her dreams.
May you find inspiration in Sara's journey.

CONTENTS

ACKNOWLEDGMENTS

I want to thank my professors from Penn State University, and especially Dr. John Haddad, Dr. Kupfer, and Dr. Simon Bronner. They have been instrumental in helping me understand and appreciate history and the study of America. I would also like to thank Heather Perez of Stockton University because she was the first person who brought Sara Spencer Washington to my attention. I spent a significant amount of time researching at the Atlantic City Free Public Library, working on my first book, *Chicken Bone Beach*, when I came across Madame Washington. The next thing you know, I asked Heather to pull research for Sara out alongside my other stacks. I want to thank Jaqueline Murillo of the Atlantic City Free Public Library for constantly digging up research for me to review. I want to thank the staff of the Charles L. Blockson Afro American Library at Temple University. I didn't thank this person in my first book, but I should have, so I want to express my sincere appreciation for my high school English teacher, Mr. Don Monaco, for helping to develop me into a skillful essay writer. He brought the gift of writing out of me in a way that I didn't realize existed. I want to thank Catherine Clement-Jenkins and Diane Borys for the time and effort put into editing and critiquing the content of the book. I wanted to thank Royston Scott, the grandson of Sara Spencer Washington, for allowing me to have a conversation with him about his grandmother that was very open and honest. I want to thank my friends and family who have supported my goals as a writer and given me constructive advice, encouragement, and support.

Most importantly, I would like to say thank you to Madame Sara Spencer Washington for living such an amazing life. The more I read about her, the more I fell in love with her. She paved the way for a multitude of women to be able to take charge of their destinies when very few people in America cared about the fate of the black race after they were freed from slavery. Sara acquired a large amount of wealth for herself, but her philanthropy and generosity toward our country deserves its rightful place in the history books.

INTRODUCTION – WHO IS SARA SPENCER WASHINGTON?

Sara Spencer Washington (June 6, 1889 – March 23, 1953) lived the American Dream on her terms. She didn't require a seat at the table because she created her own. Her parents wanted her to become a teacher, but Sara decided to study chemistry and open a hair salon. Sara's mission became to cure the hair problems of Negro women and make them more beautiful. At the age of nineteen, Sara Spencer Washington founded Apex Beauty Schools, where African-American women and men could learn about Beauty Culture and open hair salons of their own. Sara's journey is a vital piece of American history. She played an important role in demonstrating to America that black women and men possess the ability to become captains of industry, just like her white American counterparts. Madame Spencer Washington seized the opportunity to capture a market share of an emerging sector only dominated by two other African-American women. She understood the process to pursue her dream and strategically set out on a mission to duplicate her colleagues, Madame C.J. Walker and Annie Turnbo-Malone, in the beauty sector. Since very few companies in the United States took an interest in the cosmetic needs of the black American woman, the opportunity presented itself for women of color to fill the gaps and address an untapped consumer market in America and beyond. The first on record to profit from the African-American beauty sector was Madame C.J. Walker, born with the name Sarah Breedlove, who paved the way for her race. The ability of African-American women to resolve their beauty concerns bought them an avenue for independent lives during the post-slavery era. An early pioneer of the African-American beauty industry, Sara was a highly respected woman of influence and power, leading her community and creating economic growth by employing African-Americans in roles where there were limited job opportunities, giving back to Atlantic City, and conducting business internationally. People familiar with Sara stated that Madame Spencer Washington had the "Midas Touch." Everything she touched turned to gold, and seemingly every dream she imagined was made manifest. Known by others as the person who did not take no for an answer, when Madame Washington spoke, others listened. She taught those seeking to control their destiny how to acquire financial freedom while leaving a legacy with the potential of decades of longevity. Sara Spencer Washington demonstrated bravery, class, and confidence in her pursuit to build the Apex empire. Sara went from styling hair in her basement and selling cosmetics door-to-door to going public and selling millions of dollars in beauty products. Without question, as a person of color with groundbreaking ambition and drive, she experienced her share of discrimination, trials, roadblocks, and challenges as she climbed the regal ladder of success. Nevertheless, Madame Sara Spencer Washington refused to be denied access to equality for herself and other African-Americans in her community. No sooner than I learned about Sara, I instantly became captivated by her story. As I researched her journey, I became enthralled with the illustrious achievements of Apex and gathered so much research about her simply to be able to know what could have possibly happened to Apex News and Hair Company. Writing led me down the noble path of family chronicles, friendships, illness, and religion. I am in awe of Madame Sara Spencer Washington and her sheer ability to dive into the beauty business, surpassing the black women pioneers whose recipe she emulated and took it a step further by becoming a consumer market leader in the beauty industry. I love the story of Sara Spencer Washington for a variety of reasons. Her brilliance, boldness, and business savvy at such a young age is highly commendable. There are certain lessons in life that stand out for everyone, and while pursuing my Master of Business Administration, my professors painted a detailed yet broad picture of a great leader of any organization. Great leaders have a vision, and their primary job is to keep everyone within the company enthusiastic about the mission. Great leaders leave a successor and a succession plan. Madame Sara Spencer Washington is leadership at its finest, running a profitable business during the Depression. She was also a leader in her community and the only female on a civic board with all white men. Sara sued the United States government, won in real estate related cases, and organized a boycott of a restaurant refusing to serve Blacks. Sara rented an airplane and had coupons for free coal dispensed throughout Atlantic City. She groomed a successor and left an intricate will. Sara deserves an honorable place in American Studies because of her ability to accomplish, grow, and expand a profitable business in American at a turbulent and dismal time. My devotion towards communicating and preserving her legacy became so intimate that I went as far as to apply with the New Jersey Historical Preservation Office in Trenton, New Jersey, to ensure that the one remaining Apex building in Atlantic City be preserved. Boss babes of the new millennium are indebted to one of the most impressive female bosses about whom I've ever learned. African-American women employed in Corporate America continue to be viewed as second-class citizens, yet gradually break glass ceilings on income equality and stature in corporations. However, nearly ninety years ago, Sara creatively and strategically found avenues to accomplish what she wanted as the queen of Apex. She provided Blacks with employment opportunities, education, and avenues to enjoy provisions of which they were deprived. Possessing a spirit like Rosa Parks and Harriett Tubman, Madame Spencer Washington refused to succumb to those with authority and demanded that diversity and inclusion existed when it involved the business of building her company. Madame Spencer Washington inspires me to be courageous enough to trust myself to do the impossible. I am hopeful that she will have a rousing effect on individuals who hear her story. Although Washington has a historical marker in her honor and a short-film documentary about her, this body of work provides a layer of his-torical narrative and insight into the life of Madame Sara Spencer Washington that has yet to be told. My ongoing goal is to maintain the integrity of my research "as is" regarding Madame Spencer Washington. In my heart, I desire to beam her light towards the readers. The reader will get a literary journey down the road of Apex from its humble beginnings to its eventual dissolution. Apex News and Hair Company flourished most intriguingly and impressively and her contributions to society are worthy of a dignified place in history.

1

BLACK BEAUTY
CULTURE BUSINESS

The Beauty Culture industry is an important movement in African-American women's history because it was one of the first sectors of business where Blacks acquired financial freedom. My goal with including the background of the black Beauty Culture was to set a backdrop of the movement occurring in the industry when Madame Sara Spencer Washington began expanding her vision for

Apex. Historically, African-American women were denied the same employment opportunities as Whites. Their choices consisted of domestic work such as cleaning, sewing, caring for children, and cooking. As we approached the 1920s, marketing, and social attitudes towards the idea that cosmetics could assist in helping women become more attractive grew. African-Americans represented over one-tenth of the population before World War I.

Nevertheless, the beauty industry made no provisions for their distinctive hair texture or skin tones. For women of color, this made for fertile ground for entrepreneurs. Two women who were groundbreakers in this area were Annie Turnbo-Malone and Madame C.J. Walker. Madame C.J. Walker became the first female African-American self-made millionaire. She began a business in 1906 with consumer products that she used on her own hair. In the course of resolving her own hair concerns, Madame C.J. Walker developed a successful line of beauty products called the Walker System. She encouraged her customers to become part of the new-found movement that appealed mostly to Africa-American women.

Annie Turnbo-Malone was next to become independently wealthy by joining the supreme progression of creating beauty products for women of color. Turnbo-Malone started selling products under the trade name "Poro." By the 1920s, Turnbo-Malone resurrected a massive monarchy in Chicago, Illinois, and St. Louis, Missouri. Madame Sara Spencer Washington was the next giant who entered the beauty scene. African-American women are indebted to Walker and Malone for their contribution to the beauty industry and inspiring women like Madame Spencer Washington to continue down the path of Beauty Culture. Long after Madame C.J. Walker's death, Sara continued to learn, expand, and grow the Beauty Culture business. She developed a line of beauty products and equipment, exhibiting at beauty trade shows and employing Apex agents to sell her products. During the 1930s, the economic success of Apex surpassed that of both Walker and Malone. With emerging products, ideas, and possibilities, black women began to find ways to enhance their appearance. Moreover, many African-American women leaped at the chance to create a career path in the beauty industry by becoming licensed beauticians, setting up businesses in their home, or opening hair salons.

One of the most competitive and increasingly growing areas in America for the beauty giants to grow their beauty business was New York City. All three black beauty giants were doing business in Harlem. Beauty parlors became the most prevalent form of black business in Harlem during the 1920s and the 1930s. Black sociologist George Edmund Haynes, who also founded the Urban League, surveyed the neighborhood's businesses in 1921 and found 103 hairdressers compared to 63 tailors, pressers, and cleaners, and 10 to 51 barbers. Sims Bluebook, a directory of black businesses and professionals published in 1923, listed 161 beauty salons, more than any other enterprise. Combining that list with the businesses that advertised in Harlem's newspapers, the map shows the location of 199 beauty parlors operating in the 1920s. So many existed because it took relatively little capital to begin a beauty parlor business, especially if you operated it in your home, as most women in Harlem did. Of the 103 hairdressers identified by Haynes, in 1921, 46 operated out of stores and 57 from their homes. Beauty parlors also expanded because the trade provided an alternative to domestic service, an occupational choice despised by many Blacks due to the severe micromanagement of white employers.

Although most beauty parlors operated in homes, there was an outstanding presence along the street occupied by the neighborhood's businesses, particularly Seventh Avenue. Madame C.J. Walker had the most elaborate beauty parlor in Harlem during the 1920s, located at 110 West 136th Street in an intricate townhouse that she built in 1914. Her daughter occupied it in the 1920s until it became the home of a government health-care center in 1930. Also housed in the same building was Walker's beauty school. At least five other beauty schools were operating in Harlem, one of which was the Apex Beauty College located on the corner of Seventh Avenue and 135th Street, putting Sara Spencer Washington's schools and salons in direct competition with Madame C.J. Walker and other beauty schools. Sara's aggressive strategy proved worthwhile. In 1927, the *Pittsburgh Courier* reported that Sara Spencer Washington initiated a "Beauty War" by opening a string of new beauty parlors on 7th Avenue. Madame Spencer Washington was also accused of promoting an illegal form of lottery called "the numbers" in her establishments. According to a reporter from the *New York Daily News* in 1938, Apex erected a sign in the window advertising her location as a numbers headquarters. As reputation has it, beauty parlors and barbershops alike were known for generating a variety of non-beauty businesses, and it was said that Sara Spencer Washington had a beauty parlor in Harlem that became a huge hub for number-running.

Sara Spencer Washington shown standing. Two other individuals are
unidentified. (Alfred M. Heston Collection, Atlantic City Free Public Library.)

2

APEX IS BORN

"Free Yourself from Economic Slavery."
—*Sara Spencer Washington*

Sara Phillips (Washington), the daughter of Joshua and Ellen (Douglass) Philips, was born on June 6, 1889, in Norfolk, Virginia. She had two brothers, and her family was of lower-middle-class status. Madame Spencer Washington received her education at a public school in Beckley, Virginia, and then at Lincoln Preparatory School in Philadelphia, Pennsylvania. Sara also attended

Norfolk Mission College, studied Beauty Culture in York, Pennsylvania, and Advanced Chemistry at Columbia University. In 1905, Madame Washington worked as a dressmaker while also employed to perform domestic work. While living in York, Sara Spencer Washington worked as a personal maid for a wealthy family. The golden moment began when Sara's mistress's salon appointment was canceled, and she asked Sara to style her hair instead. Sara's mistress was so pleased with Sara's work; she continued the role of her mistress's hairdresser. Sara proceeded to study Beauty Culture in York, Pennsylvania and moved to Philadelphia, where she became a leading barber and received her Bachelor of Science in Business Administration from Norfolk Mission College in Norfolk, Virginia. The combination of skills in business and chemistry prepared Madame Washington for her destiny. Sara and her mother moved to Atlantic City for the sake of her mother's health. In the early twentieth century, it was publicized that the salt in the ocean air was beneficial to improving health. Sara relocated in 1913 while still married to Isaac Washington, whom she wedded during World War I, but they separated in 1919. Once Sara arrived and settled in, Madame Spencer Washington began styling hair in her home. She also proceeded to experiment with chemicals to produce hair and beauty products. Once Sara established enough items to sell, she traveled door-to-door on the north side of Atlantic City, showing women how to apply her beauty cosmetics and creating customers. During the early 1900s, the black population in Atlantic City resided on the Northside. Additionally, door-to-door marketing became a useful and effective way of promoting consumer goods in the United States during the early 1900s. As Sara visited her neighbors, the community embraced her enthusiasm and confidence. Potential customers were excited to have the chance to purchase makeup and hair products since women of color had few choices in consumer goods tailored for their complexion and hair texture. Sara offered solutions and a needed boost in self-esteem to women who desired cosmetic options suited for their beauty concerns. After years of hard work and dedication to her craft, in 1919, Sara founded Apex News and Hair Company. Apex News and Hair Company was located on the corner of 1725 Arctic Avenue in Atlantic City, New Jersey. The news division of Apex truly made Sara a leader in her market segment, providing relevant and current information on the beauty industry and creating a larger voice in black America. It proved to be a viable marketing concept also utilized by her predecessors in the industry.

As a result of the continued growth of Apex News and Hair Company, Madame Sara Spencer Washington opened a manufacturing location and warehouse in Atlantic City and a salon and beauty school in New York City. Adding to the layers of Apex News and Hair Company was the opening of Apex Laboratories. Sara's educational background in Chemistry was exercised during the early days of Apex. Justifiably, instead of spending time in the laboratories inventing new products, Madame Spencer Washington devoted her energy to her vision. Over the years, Apex Laboratories invented hundreds of consumer goods and earned patents. One of Sara's patents was for a hair curl-removal system, which she marketed nationally, using her own ideas to promote her product. "Glossatina" guaranteed a long-lasting smooth luster to hair, along with the use of specialized combs and brushes.

Apex News and Hair Company provided employment opportunities to African-Americans in diverse roles on every level, from Vice-Presidents to Chemists, even earning a profit in the 1930s during the Depression. Madame Washington utilized this economic circumstance in the United States to put her business savvy to work. From the start of

Apex, Madame Washington made it a habit to keep debt lean by paying cash for almost everything as often as she could afford to. If Sara had an outstanding balance on loan, she paid them off quickly. In fact, Madame Washington promoted her Apex Beauty Schools by encouraging potential recruits to learn about Beauty Culture and create a "depression-proof" business. Women and a few men of color who became licensed beauticians opened hair salons, filling a void for their own race by providing goods and services overlooked by mainstream corporations. In addition to America, the vacuum of black hair care and beauty products existed in other countries besides the United States. Madame Washington seized the opportunity to grow the Apex Empire by expanding internationally and introducing citizens of South Africa and other Caribbean islands to her products, increasing enrollment at her beauty schools. Sara and other officers of her staff traveled internationally, building relationships and

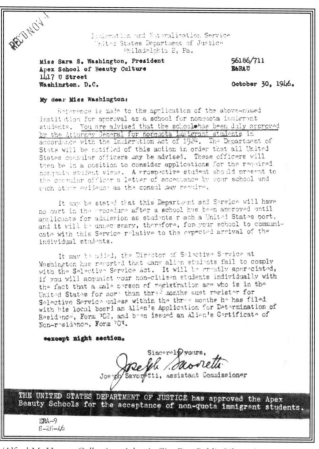

Immigration and Naturalization Service
United States Department of Justice
Philadelphia 2, Pa.

Miss Sara S. Washington, President   56186/711
Apex School of Beauty Culture   E&RAU
1417 U Street
Washington, D.C.   October 30, 1946.

My dear Miss Washington:

Reference is made to the application of the above-named institution for approval as a school for nonquota immigrant students. You are advised that the school has been duly approved by the Attorney General for nonquota immigrant students in accordance with the Immigration Act of 1924. The Department of State will be notified of this action in order that all United States consular officers may be advised. These officers will then be in a position to consider applications for the required nonquota student visas. A prospective student should present to the consular officer a letter of acceptance by your school and such other evidence as the consul may require.

It may be stated that this Department and Service will have no part in the procedure after a school has been approved until applicants for admission as students reach a United States port, and it will be unnecessary, therefore, for your school to communicate with this Service relative to the expected arrival of the individual students.

It may be added, the Director of Selective Service at Washington has reported that many alien students fail to comply with the Selective Service Act. It will be greatly appreciated, if you will acquaint your non-citizen students individually with the fact that a male person of registration age who is in the United States for more than three months must register for Selective Service unless within the three months he has filed with his local board an Alien's Application for Determination of Residence, Form 302, and been issued an Alien's Certificate of Non-residence, Form 303.

*except night section.

Sincerely yours,

Joseph Savoretti

Joseph Savoretti, Assistant Commissioner

THE UNITED STATES DEPARTMENT OF JUSTICE has approved the Apex Beauty Schools for the acceptance of non-quota immigrant students.

ERA-9
8-26-46

(Alfred M. Heston Collection, Atlantic City Free Public Library.)

learning how to broaden their product lines and open schools. Sara also assisted many of her international students with acquiring temporary visas to attend Apex Beauty Schools, many of which returned to their homelands and sold beauty products as Apex agents or opened hair salons. Madame Washington also gave away scholarships to attend Apex Beauty College.

One aspect of Sara's business that aided in her ability to retain customers was using her news division to publish instruction manuals on how to apply her products effectively and exercise proper hair care and maintenance. She touted Apex's success to the quality of its products and sound business principles for running the organization. Madame Washington also gave credit to her scientists at Apex Laboratories for developing over two-hundred products, admitting that she created only the first two. Alongside pamphlets on how to use her goods, she advised the reader on the importance of cleanliness and grooming. Sara wrote about how to resolve problems like dandruff, dry scalp, and getting stains out. Apex Laboratories also produced several household products such as floor wax, furniture polish, insect spray, machine oil, cooking flavors such as vanilla, white shoe cleaner, perfume, starch, cough syrup, and glass cleaner.

Apex Laboratories Product List

Product	Price
Apex Glossatina	$0.50
Apex Scalp Cream	$0.50
Apex Skin Bleach	$0.60
Apex Special Hair Pomade	$0.50
Apex Pomade	$0.35
Apex Cocoanut Oil Shampoo	$0.50
Apex All Purpose Wax	$1.00
Apex Tar Oil	$0.50
Apex Hair Tonic Lotion	$0.50
Apex Cream Shampoo (with Lanolin)	$0.75
Almond Perfume Lotion	$0.50
Apex Skin Balm	$0.50
Apex Face Cream	$0.35
Apex Deodorant Cream	$0.50
Apex Cologne	$0.50
Apex Cream Hair Tonic	$0.50
Apex Rose Oil	$0.35
Apex Lustoria	$0.50
Edible Olive Oil	$1.00
Apex Beauty Soap	$0.10
Apex Lath-O (Soap)	$0.25
Apex Solid Powder Compact	$0.25
Apex Brushless Shaving Cream	$0.35
Apex Bubble Bath	$0.60
Apex Shaving Cream, Lather	$0.40
Apex All Purpose Cream	$0.50
Apex Lipstick	$1.00
Apex Cream Rouge	$0.50
Apex Face Powder	$0.40

Apex Dry Rogue.........................$0.50
Apex Cream Rogue $0.50
Apex Eye Brow Pencil....................$0.20
Apex Medicated Skin Cream $0.50
Apex Cough Syrup.......................$0.60
Apex Witch Hazel $0.50
Apex Liniment..........................$0.50
Apex Nail Polish........................$0.15
Apex Polish Remover $0.15
Apex Cuticle Remover $0.15
Tincture Green Soap $0.75
Apex Floor Wax $0.50
Apex Mineral Oil.......................$0.60
Apex Glass Gleaner $0.50
Apex White Shoe Cleaner.................$0.25
Apex Tooth Powder $0.25
Apex Shampoo Oil.......................$1.00
Apex Cream Furniture Polish...............$0.50
Apex Mouth Wash $0.35
Nylon Comb & Brush Sets $1.98
Nylon Hair Brush $2.50
Coarse Tooth Long Handle Comb............$1.25
Dressing Comb $0.75
Wavesetta Marcel Comb..................$0.50
Tapering Barber Comb....................$0.50
Heavy Brass Comb.......................$2.25
Apex Brass Comb........................$2.25
Straightening Comb......................$1.50
Small Neck and Temple Comb...............$0.60
Light Weight Comb......................$1.25
Electric Straightening Comb $3.50
Hot Oil Electric Heater $2.50
Pressure Shampoo Spray...................$2.00
Glass Oil Spray..........................$1.00
Deluxe Hand Hair Dryer...................$18.00
Master Violet Ray........................$16.50
Hump Marcel Iron.......................$3.98
French Pressing & Marcel Iron...............$4.00
Gas Stove $5.00
Pressing tongs..........................$1.95

Pressing and Marcel Waving Iron $3.50
Triangle Veils $0.30
Oster "Model B" Clippers $4.00
Hair Clipper. $2.00
Hair Clipper. $4.75
Barber Shears $3.00
Black Diamond Razor $3.50
Sponge Rubber Make-Up Puff. $0.20
Black Hair Stick. $0.75
Economical Tooth Brush $0.15
Nylon Tooth Brush $0.40
Godefroy Hair Coloring. $1.25

(Source: Atlantic City Free Public Library, Heston
Collection, Washington, Sara S., "World's Finest Beauty
Preparations and their Use." Apex News and Hair Company,
Inc.)

On June 7, 1927, Apex Company was chartered as a corporation in New Jersey. The authorized capitalization was $100,000. By the mid-1930s, the Apex Beauty Products Company was the largest New Jersey black-owned and black-ran businesses and one of the nation's leading black manufacturing companies. As early as 1933, Madame Spencer Washington was advertising her beauty cosmetics in an African trade journal called, *Bantu World*. *Bantu World* was a newspaper created and published in 1932 by Bertram

Paver, a white ex-farmer from Johannesburg, South Africa. *Bantu World*'s intended audience was the black middle-class elite. Paver modeled *Bantu World* after British tabloids. The newspaper had national distribution and each issue comprised of twenty pages, the majority of which were written in English and the remaining in a mixture of indigenous languages.

To effectively acquire market share, Apex also employed a white European man named "Jolly" Jack Benard as an agent in Johannesburg, South Africa. This was a contrast from Apex's routine marketing strategy in the United States, where all of Apex's agents were black. Nevertheless, promotional efforts in Africa continued to be targeted towards women of color with similar hair and cosmetic concerns. Apex even changed the verbiage in some of their advertisements to the South-African language. A native South-African businessman praised Apex in magazine articles he wrote as being the first all-negro company to do business in South Africa. *Bantu World* magazine wrote several articles about Sara and the Apex empire boasting about their success with an emphasis on uplifting the black race. Simultaneously, Apex's advertisements were met with criticism, and counter-articles surfaced about the use of face powders and skin-bleachers. Skin-bleaching has been in existence since the Victorian Age, used by white women to demonstrate "purity," but in terms of Africa and the United States, it has often been judged for creating self-image issues amongst darker women.

Conversely, favorable commentary was written by an African woman named Rilda Marta, who traveled to the United States to study medicine but decided instead to study Beauty Culture. She wrote articles encouraging women from South Africa to use beauty and hair products to enhance their appearance. She concurred with beauty giants such as Madame C.J. Walker and Madame Spencer

Pictured standing is Sara Spencer Washington on Missouri Avenue Beach (Chicken Bone Beach) in Atlantic City, New Jersey. Missouri Avenue Beach was a segregated beach in Atlantic City during the 1920s through the 1960s. (Alfred M. Heston Collection, Atlantic City Free Public Library.)

Washington that beauty products and hair styling provided a sense of self-respect and confidence lacking in African women.

During the peak of Apex's economic growth in 1937, Sara's mother, Ellen Hunter, died after only being sick for three days. Ellen Hunter served as the treasurer of Apex. She was survived by one son, Frank Phillips; two nieces, Mrs. Maud Turnage of Berkley,

West Virginia, and Mrs. Verna Joshua Wynn; a granddaughter, Miss Ida Ellen Phillips of Reading, Pennsylvania; and Joan Cross Washington, grandniece. In memory of her mother, Madame Washington opened the Ellen Hunter School for Girls, a place where young ladies learned how to become entrepreneurs.

Unfortunately, during the same year of the passing of Ellen Hunter, Sara Spencer Washington fell down the stairs and injured herself, sustaining a dislocated vertebra, while visiting the home of Dr. And Mrs. Lylburn Downing. When Sara left the Downings, she traveled to Hot Springs, Arkansas, where physicians treated her in her hotel room. As a result of her injury, Sara began using a cane to maintain mobility. Regardless of her tragedy and health, Madame Sara Spencer Washington forged ahead to continue to grow her legacy. Her commitment to assisting her race in acquiring economic freedom prompted her to create an annual campaign to attract new employees. To effectively communicate Apex's employment drive, Madame Washington created the slogan, "Free yourself from economic slavery," to attract Blacks to apply for jobs with Apex and encourage them to pursue economic independence. This led Sara to designate the month of July "Progress Month" in honor of the 750th anniversary of the Emancipation Proclamation. Sara stated, "The time has long since arrived when Negro business enterprises should be more energetic in their desires to gain greater patronage from their people and, in turn, employ more race workers." Apex's job fair continued to be an annual event every July.

By 1938, Apex opened ten Apex Beauty Culture Schools across the United States. Apex Beauty Schools were in Baltimore, Maryland; New York City, New York; Atlantic City, New Jersey; Washington D.C.; Richmond, Virginia; Chicago, Illinois; Philadelphia, Pennsylvania; and Atlanta, Georgia. The interest in Apex Beauty College traveled beyond America, allowing Apex to offer a scholarship to Mrs. Ekanem, a schoolteacher from Nigeria, West Africa. Through the assistance of the foreign mission of the Salvation Army, Mrs. Ekanem attended Apex Beauty College in New York City. Mrs. Ekanem traveled to the United States with her husband, Dr. Joseph Ekanem, a physician. Mrs. Ekanem recognized the growing popularity in hair modernization and styling practiced in America was more desirable in Africa.

The popularity of Apex Beauty Schools increasingly grew over the early years of their existence. Capacity crowds often came to open houses sponsored by Apex Beauty College to watch demonstrations. Many black women in America moved to cities where Apex Schools existed to earn their certification. Students from New Mexico, Florida, North Carolina, Virginia, Massachusetts, Maryland, and New Jersey graduated from the Apex College of Scientific Beauty Culture in Atlantic City.

APEX SCHOOL LOCATIONS:

N.E. Corner of 47th and South Parkway
Chicago, Illinois

163 West Kinney Street
Newark, New Jersey

895 Fulton Street
Brooklyn, New York

200 West 135th Street
New York, New York

Broad and South Street
Philadelphia, Pennsylvania

1726 Arctic Avenue
Atlantic City, New Jersey

Auburn Ave. and Butler Street
Atlanta, Georgia

212 East Clay Street
Richmond, Virginia

1854 Pennsylvania Avenue
Baltimore, Maryland

(Source: Atlantic City Free Public Library, Heston Collection, Washington, Sara S., "World's Finest Beauty Preparations and their Use." Apex News and Hair Company, Inc.)

3

APEX GROWS INTO
AN EMPIRE

"We at Apex have grown with Atlantic City."
—Sara Spencer Washington

Madame Washington has been referred to as one of the most important business executives in the black community during the height of her company's growth. She owned one of the largest Negro-owned and staffed manufacturing companies in the United States. By 1946, the impressive expansion of Apex resulted in phenomenal job growth. Sara Spencer Washington created jobs for 45,000 agents in the United States, South Africa, the Caribbean, and the West Indies. Madame Washington employed chemists, laboratory technicians, office workers, teachers, sales representatives, stenographers, clerks, and managers, manufacturing hundreds of products at her plant. Madame Spencer Washington bought a fleet of Apex trucks for deliveries of raw materials to her plant daily. Apex's growing business needs led to the acquisition of four warehouses, all located in Atlantic City, and filled with supplies required to produce and package finished goods. Apex's international reach was also very profitable, as Apex sold more products in the city of Port-de-Prince, Haiti, than the entire state of New Jersey during the early 1950s. Haiti was one of Apex's most lucrative markets. Madame Washington morphed into a colossus, holding a position in the beauty industry equivalent to the financial profits of her white counterparts, such as Estee Lauder and Elisabeth Arden. Madame Spencer Washington earned the respect of both Whites and Blacks in Atlantic City as a result of her leadership as a sound and prosperous businesswoman. As equally awe-inspiring as her leadership of Apex was her civic contributions along her journey. Her work was purposed with the ability to have a voice to advocate equality for the Negro race. Her generous heart, brave spirit, and fearless confidence knew no bounds. Washington's successes began to receive notoriety by outside organizations as well. Most notably, Sara was honored at the 1939 New York World's Fair as one of the "Most Distinguished Businesswomen." Sara's drive, work ethic, and effective business strategy resulted in Apex Enterprises grossing more than one million in sales this year. To put the financial achievements of Madame Spencer Washington into perspective, when you adjust inflation, $1,000,000 in 1946 is equal to $13,804,010.99 in 2019. (dollar-times.com) Madame Spencer Washington's willingness to assist the underprivileged in acquiring equal opportunity to build wealth attracted prosperity for Apex. In Apex's promotional and informational brochures, Sara shares with readers how she grew the Apex empire, saying, "I have built up the business which I head by dealing honestly with the public at all times. I give our customers the best value possible for the money spent. I don't recommend any product for use by the public, which has not been thoroughly tried and proved and which I would not use on my own hair and skin."

Sara's longest legacy, the Apex Beauty Colleges, increased its enrollment at a rapid pace as people of color sought to establish independent economic footing. Three-thousand students were graduating from Apex Beauty Schools annually in twelve states and three foreign countries during the 1940s. Public demonstrations of hair techniques drew hundreds of people to witness the teachings at Apex Beauty School. Also, amid the phenomenal growth and success of the hard-working empress of the Apex empire, Sara married Shumpert Logan on October 6, 1944, a gentleman who Madame Spencer Washington had been friends with for years. Shortly after their nuptials, he became an employee of Apex.

Washington made acquisitions that continued to thrive over the years. One of which was a golf course that Madame Spencer Washington invested in after encountering discrimination at the establishment. In the late 1940s, Sara opened Apex Golf Course and charitably made it available for use by all races of any economic status. Sara may have been one of the first African-American women in America to purchase a golf course. The Apex Golf Club, which later became known as the Ponoma Golf Club, hosted the Centennial National Open Professional and Amateur Tournament. The golf course has nine holes, and golfers can play at the par thirty-four course with 2,426 yardages.

Pictured here Sara Spencer Washington in a white coat, left of center, along with members and visitors of Apex Golf Course and Country Club. (Alfred M. Heston Collection, Atlantic City Free Public Library.)

People shown enjoying Apex Golf Course, which was owned by Sara Spencer Washington. Washington was one of the first African-Americans to own a golf course in the nation. (Alfred M. Heston Collection, Atlantic City Free Public Library.)

People shown enjoying Apex Golf Course. (Alfred M. Heston Collection, Atlantic City Free Public Library.)

More people shown enjoying Apex Golf Course. (Alfred M. Heston Collection, Atlantic City Free Public Library.)

Madame Spencer Washington also founded a nursing home called Apex Rest in Atlantic City, New Jersey. Apex Rest was located on the corner of Indiana and Ontario Avenue. It was a fifteen-year-old facility in Atlantic City used primarily by company employees but was still open to the public. Recreational facilities included an auditorium often converted into a dance floor from a basketball court. Apex Rest was a luxurious bed and breakfast offering tennis courts, pavilion dancing, croquet, and private rooms. While staying, guests could enjoy fresh fruits and vegetables, eggs, and milk that came from Sara's farm, Apex Farm. A portion of this land was benevolently donated to provide summer camps for youth. Apex Farm was a 120-acre tract of land in Egg Harbor, New Jersey. Sara also owned Apex Drug Store, which was located at 1800 Arctic Avenue, Indiana, which also provided luncheonette and delivery service.

Along with building a solid corporation with subsidiaries, Madame Washington made time to participate in civic duties and philanthropy. A regal pillar of her community, Sara was an active member of the Atlantic City Board of Trade for many years. She was also elected to the Atlantic County Republican Committee in 1938 and served as a New Jersey delegate at the 1940 Republican National Convention. Historically, there was a time in America when registering as a Republican meant you were a part of the Democratic Party. She took on leadership roles as the president of the Northside Business and Professional Women's Club in Atlantic City, Chair of the Living Relatives, Chair of the Industrial Department of the New Jersey State Federation of Colored Women's Clubs, a member of the Atlantic City Board of Trade, and during World War II, she filled the position of secretary and treasurer of the New Jersey Welfare Commission on the Conditions of Urban

Colored Populations. Sara's philanthropic reach to elevate the plight of the black race in America extended in every direction in which Madame Washington could partake. In 1944, Sara bought a $10,000 War Bond in connection with a nation-wide campaign to sell $2,000,000 in War Bonds to honor Harriet Tubman.

Consequently, Sara was asked to honor the late Tubman by breaking a champagne bottle at the launching of the SS Harriet Tubman. Many also told stories of Madame Spencer Washington buying carloads of coal, renting a plane to fly over the Atlantic City, and dropping the coupons for free coal. During the Great Depression, access to this resource was invaluable for surviving, especially in the winter months.

Despite Madame Spencer Washington's tremendous wealth, she continued to endure racism but addressed it with dignity and class. One encounter of discrimination occurred while Madame Spencer Washington went shopping at Wanamaker's department store in Philadelphia, Pennsylvania. Opening in 1876, Wanamaker's was one of the first department stores in America. An anchor of Philadelphia's central shopping district, it attracted wealthy shoppers. A young white salesgirl working in the fur department that day was said to have noticed Madame Spencer Washington's presence but chose to blatantly ignore her and help white customers. Except for Madame Spencer Washington's skin color, she fit the profile to shop there just based on her attire, which consisted of a silk brocade dress and an elegant tailored wool coat, leather handbag, and flawless hair and make-up. At least as far as this salesgirl was concerned. Sara Spencer Washington browsed around visibly bothered by the lack of courtesy shown but remained poised and patient.

Meanwhile, in walks the supervisor who immediately recognized Mrs. Spencer Washington, presented himself, and said,

"Mrs. Washington, back so soon?" She replied, "I'd like to get one more if I may." Sara was referring to a mink coat. It was apparent to the supervisor what may have taken place with the salesgirl and she was ordered to get another mink for Sara. Madame Washington promptly wrote a check for $4,600. In 1946, the cost of an average home in the United States was equal to what Sara spent that afternoon. Pricey for certain but Madame Spencer Washington made her point very clear when she had been treated so rudely. This is reminiscent of the story of Oprah Winfrey shopping in the Hermes store in Switzerland in 2005 when seeking to purchase a $38,000 handbag. Sadly, racial inequality and prejudice remains prevalent globally despite the many decades of economic progression for people of color. One thing was for certain, Madame Sara Spencer Washington was a powerful influence who spoke out against racism and acted when necessary to defend her race. She sued a restaurant once in Atlantic City that refused to serve her and bought out another one for the night and invited her friends.

Madame Spencer Washington also met challenges of inclusivity when entering women into the infamous annual Easter Parade on the Boardwalk in Atlantic City, which ultimately led to the start of the African-American Easter Parade on the Northside of Atlantic City. Atlantic City was coined for a city of beauty and glamour from its early days of existence. It is the birthplace of the Miss America pageant, and for decades beauty parades were big business. A person who tore down barriers to keep African-Americans involved in events in Atlantic City, Sara entered three young ladies into the widely-known and attended Easter Parade. In 1942, Madame Washington spent an exhilarating, long day preparing her girls for the parade and took them shopping at Blum's Department in Philadelphia, specifically advising the store manager to select the best dresses, coats, shoes, accessories, and suits for their big debut. The manager obliged Madame Washington's every request, knowing full well that this tall, classy, confident woman was able to add as many zeros to a check to Blum's Department for anything in the store. Sara was beauty royalty, recognized by those who mattered everywhere she traveled. Regardless of how dignified and beautiful the African-American contestants were, they were over-looked for even an honorable mention. It was at that time that Madame Washington decided to create an Easter Parade on the Northside where the beauty of African-American women could be recognized. At fifty-seven years old, Madame Sara Spencer Washington achieved massive success. Her level of fortune was noticed and admired by the black communities in America and beyond. She was Atlantic City's golden girl who accomplished anything she put her mind to, with room to grow.

4

SARA BECOMES ILL

"Father Divine Makes Me Feel Better than Medicine."
—Sara Spencer Washington

Madame Washington suffered a stroke in 1943, and it was at that time she was diagnosed with diabetes. Her doctors gave her medication and advised her to make changes to her busy work schedule, especially as it involved her activities with Father Divine and his church. Medication for the treatment of diabetes was not as advanced as it is today. Many people treated for diabetes in the 1940s were not given a long time to live once diagnosed. At the time that Sara was diagnosed, she was a loyal and dedicated member of Father Divine's church. While Sara was attending Columbia University in New York City, she became inquisitive about the teachings of Father Divine. Father Divine became famous during the Great Depression by the charity of his outreach ministry. He fed the hungry, both blacks and whites, and drew a following of thousands. Born George Baker, who named himself Reverend Major Jealous Divine, grew up in the South but relocated to Long Island in 1919, where he began distributing books on New Thought. Father Divine's teachings were like the believers of Christian Science. Most significantly, he was at the forefront of the fight for racial equality, founding and heading the International Peace Mission, which was referred to as a melting pot of Americans, both black and white, who were dissatisfied with popular ideology. After attending a meeting, Madame

Spencer Washington was sold on his principles and, through the years, became a loyal supporter of his causes. Father Divine's racial integration in his Peace Mission movement was revolutionary at a time in America when most congregations were segregated.

When questioned by the press about her health at a banquet in Philadelphia, Sara stated that she was overcoming diabetes. "Through the aid of Father Divine, I am gradually overcoming diabetes that has virtually suppressed me. Father Divine makes me feel better than medicine" (The Baltimore Afro-Americas). It's possible that Madame Washington was given medical advice about her healthcare that she chose to disregard. The issue of her health stayed on the media's radar from the moment the news was released. Sara Spencer Washington was a very public and recognized figure, especially in African-American publications, and she and her closest family members remained in the news for decades. They appeared in the "high society" section of newspapers and magazines published mostly in publications such as *Ebony, Jet, Sepia, Color*, the *Philadelphia Tribune, Baltimore Afro-American News*, and *Atlantic City Free Press*. Sara suffered another stroke in 1947, which caused her to be paralyzed on her entire right side and lose her speech. It was at that time that her doctors realized that she failed to take the medication prescribed to her in 1943. As it turns out, speculations about Sara's health in the media may have carried some legitimacy.

As a result of her declining health, Sara began to set things in place to alleviate other work responsibilities. Madame Washington decided to franchise almost all her beauty schools, offering them to the current management and staff, disabling her from being engrossed in every aspect of her Apex empire. Sara appointed Lillian Robinson as supervisor of all her Apex Beauty Colleges, assigning her the responsibility of creating constructive programs that would enhance the school's curriculum. In this role, Mrs. Robinson would travel throughout the United States and to foreign countries. Mrs. Lillian Robinson started work with Apex as the superintendent of Apex Beauty College in Philadelphia, Pennsylvania. The most important girl to play a vital role in the success and legacy of the Apex empire was Madame Washington's niece, Joan Cross Washington. Sara adopted her niece due to personal family matters, but since Sara didn't have any children of her own, the arrangement was ideal. Miss Joan Cross Washington began the process of becoming the heiress of the Apex empire by working alongside Madame Washington, learning everything about the Beauty Culture business.

In 1944, Sara Spencer Washington purchased the Brigantine Hotel from Father Divine and the Divinities for $22,000. The Brigantine Hotel, which is now the Legacy Vacation Club, is in Brigantine, New Jersey. As a result of purchasing the Brigantine Hotel,

Madame Spencer Washington broke her own rule of paying off debt fairly within a few years of acquisition. In the case of the transaction with Father Divine, ownership proved to be a small blemish on Madame Washington's liquid enterprise. Father Divine and his followers bought the $750,000 hotel for $70,000. The United States government took over the hotel to house the military during the war, leaving the beautiful building in horrible condition. After the military was done using it, Madame Washington purchased it from the "Divinities" for $22,000. Also, she planned to approach the United States government to request that they restore the property to the condition it was in before its military use. As a result of Madame Washington's action, the relationship with what was referred to by the *Baltimore Afro-Americans* newspaper as a "cult," the Divinities stopped treating Sara the same as they did in the beginning. Although Madame Washington's relationship with Father Divine and the Divinities changed, she asked them to sell her the inventory in the Brigantine Hotel.

In March 1953, Madame Washington was hospitalized at Atlantic City Hospital. According to the doctors, Sara's illness was triggered by her diabetic condition. Unfortunately, on this occasion, she would not be returning to her home to continue expanding and maintaining her Apex legacy. Aware that Sara's outlook was grim, her husband and daughter were by her side. The press did not waste any time reporting her critical condition and questioning the cause of her illness. Sara's other family members living in Atlantic City, Joshua Wynn and Mrs. Vera Gosnell from Baltimore, Maryland, were also by her side. Sara passed in Atlantic City Hospital surrounded by loved ones on March 23, 1953. She was sixty-three years old. Private funeral services were held at John Carter's funeral home on Baltic and New York Avenues in Atlantic City, New Jersey. Sara's husband, Mr. Logan, spoke with the

Though unconfirmed, research has led to the belief that some of the people on the right are family members. (Alfred M. Heston Collection, Atlantic City Free Public Library.)

Three unidentified ladies with Sara Spencer Washington on the far right. (Alfred M. Heston Collection, Atlantic City Free Public Library.)

Baltimore Afro-American newspaper after her passing, stating that he and Sara had eight years of a perfect marriage and had been friends for years. Mr. Logan also mentioned that they had a lot in common, although he did not share her belief in Christian Science. Nonetheless, he attended services with her on more than one occasion.

Being the savvy businesswoman that Sara Spencer Washington was, not only had she groomed a successor for Apex, she also created a detailed will that included her funeral plans down to her attire. As requested, Sara was laid to rest wearing a gray lace dress, silver slippers, a pearl necklace, and an orchid in her hand while lying in estate. She also petitioned a funeral that would cost no more than one thousand dollars. Madame Sara Spencer Washington is buried in Pleasantville Cemetery in Pleasantville, New Jersey, beside her mother, Mrs. Ellen Hunter, and her brother, Frank Phillips. Pleasantville, New Jersey, is on the outskirts of Atlantic City. After

Madame Washington's death, newspapers continued to raise skepticism that her rapidly declining health was due to her unwillingness to follow the doctors' orders. The headlines read, "Could Madame Spencer Washington have prolonged her life had she follow the directions of her doctors for treatment?"

Madame Sara Spencer Washington's estate was valued at $602,024.95, according to an appraisal prepared about seven months after her death. Almost fifty percent of her estate included shares of stock in Apex. Sara had cash of nearly $200,000 deposited in banks, and the remainder consisted of real estate, goods, and jewelry. Sara's daughter, Miss Joan Cross Washington, became the new president of Apex News and Hair Company and inherited fifty-one percent of Apex's stock. The remaining stock was given to other family members and dedicated employees, who also comprised the board of the company. The other forty-nine percent was divided amongst relatives and employees as follows: Sara's husband Shumpert Logan and cousins Verna Goshnell and Joshua Wynn all received ten percent each; six percent interest went to Ida Johnson, another cousin; Beatrice Cannady, office manager and secretary for twenty-four years; and Archie Morgan, Sara's business manager of twenty-eight years received seven percent. Additionally, cash of ten-thousand dollars was given to the same relatives who received percentage interests in Apex. Sara also gave increments of $500 to a childhood friend, her housekeeper, and a host of other relatives and friends.

Joan Cross Washington received the bulk of Madame Washington's goods, including the home on Arctic Avenue and furnishings, furs, jewelry, life insurance annuities, and residual of the estate. The will was established on April 16, 1947, six years before her passing. Critical to the legacy of the business was the fact that the will included a notice that those who received stock of Apex could not sell, mortgage, transfer, or give it away to outsiders but must be sold to other Apex stockholders. If a stockholder dies, they must bequeath it to a surviving stockholder. When the last survivor dies, Apex Companies must buy the stock at book value. Properties owned by Madame Washington were valued as Apex Laboratories ($20,000), Apex Rest and Tourist ($50,000), Ellen Hunter Memorial Home for Girls ($18,000), Apex Drug Store ($21,000), Apex building in Philadelphia ($70,000), and the Brigantine Hotel ($150,000). A total of five people were willed the hotel. Before Sara's death, she was falling behind in property taxes on the Brigantine Hotel. After her death, property taxes were still in arrears, with a threat of foreclosure on the Brigantine Hotel. Despite this, they managed to keep the hotel afloat, though ultimately renaming it the Legacy Resort.

Shortly after Sara's passing, multiple organizations hosted events to honor Madame Sara Spencer Washington for her contributions. Shortly after Sara's death in 1953, the

National Beauty Culturists League held a fellowship tea during their histrionic pageant dedicated to the late mogul in Philadelphia. Sara's widow, Mr. Shumpert Logan, and Mr. Archie Morgan, the business manager of Apex News and Hair Company, gave remarks. A Sara Spencer Stamp Drive took place in February 1953, and the Apex Golf Club was sold and renamed Sandale Country Club. The Apex alumni gave a memorial luncheon for Madame Spencer Washington in 1958. In the 1970s, Vernon and Regina Truitt bought Sandale Country Club, gave it a cosmetic upgrade, and planted over 400 trees, renaming it Ponoma Golf Course. The golf course was passed down to their daughters Pam and Glenda. Their nephew, Bruce Ritchie, was also employed to assist.

5

APEX WITH HEIRESS JOAN

"The Growth of Apex reads like fiction."
—*The Philadelphia Tribune*

Joan Cross-Washington was born on May 28, 1927, in Atlantic City, New Jersey. Joan is the daughter of William and Verna Washington Gosnell, cousins of Madame Sara Spencer Washington. The late Spencer Washington wanted to ensure that her adopted daughter received a quality education, both in and outside of the walls of the regal empire of Apex News and Hair Company. Therefore,

Joan attended Sedalia under the tutelage of Dr. Charlotte Brown, Northfield School for Girls in Massachusetts, then Howard and Boston University. After Sara's passing, Apex News and Hair Company continued to prosper and expand under the leadership of heiress Joan Cross Washington for the first few years. The media wrote articles praising Joan's success in her new role as Apex News and Hair Company's second president. In 1954, Apex News and Hair Company experienced one of their biggest years in sales and growth in attendance at Apex Beauty Schools. Students traveled from around the country, to attend one of the prestigious Apex Beauty Colleges. One newspaper referred to Joan as, "The Young Queen of the Apex Empire," while other publications questioned the vitality and health of Apex after Sara's death. Apex News and Hair Company produced new products and acquired patents, one of which was the Liquid Press. The Liquid Press was a phenomenal greaseless pressing compound in liquid form, used in conjunction with the hot comb. The Apex Liquid Press drastically eliminated the oily feel of hair straightened with products currently available on the market. This innovative creation was first presented to professional beauty operators at a clinic of the New York State Beauticians Association in New York City. Joan Cross-Washington also opened a not-for-profit research laboratory where the focus was to thoroughly and thoughtfully examine issues and needs of skin and hair problems of the black race. Efforts of this caliber are what truly set Apex apart from other organizations because very few companies in the United States were investing their resources into the beauty concerns of Blacks despite the potential for millions of dollars in sales.

Along with record-breaking revenues experienced by Apex News and Hair Company, major changes began to occur within Apex and in Miss Washington's personal life. In less than one year after Madame Spencer Washington's death, Joanne married Holton Hayes. Hayes was a recent new hire of Apex News and Hair Company. After the marriage, Holton Hayes took a position as Executive Vice-President in 1955. Mr. and Mrs. Hayes started a family, and Joan began selling equipment at Apex Rest, noted as a mecca for the nation's high society, and built a $50,000 ranch-style home on the property. *Ebony Magazine* was invited to Hayes's new home, where Mrs. Joan Hayes gave an exclusive tour, showing off their new, gorgeous house. *Ebony Magazine*'s interview with the Hayes family included discussion about Apex and work-family balance. Additionally, in keeping with Madame Sara Spencer Washington's philanthropic work in Atlantic City, the Hayes's donated funds to the Atlantic City Hospital to build an entire maternity ward. At the time of this gesture, they had already given birth to two of their three children.

In 1956, after years of Madame Spencer Washington's effort to gain equal access to pageant festivities in Atlantic City, under the leadership of Joan Washington-Hayes, Apex entered a float in the Miss America Pageant Parade held annually during Labor Day week. This was the first time in the history of the competition that Negros participated. Also, Apex News and Company played a crucial role in getting the very first African-American contestant in the Miss America pageant. After twenty-nine years of not allowing African-American women to be a part of the event, Joan Washington-Hayes and Ballatine Beer Company combined their efforts, entering a float in the infamous opening parade. The Miss America Pageant started in September of 1921 as an option for generating business in Atlantic City during the post-summer season. Atlantic City produced massive amounts of tourists and, ultimately, plenty of financial gain from June through September. Fortunately, the pageant attracted more than 100,000 attendees to watch contestants parade along the Atlantic

City Boardwalk in bathing suits. The first woman crowned Miss America was Margaret Gorman, a sixteen-year-old from Washington D.C. Although the Miss America pageant has been in existence now for almost a hundred years, it was suspended during the Great Depression from 1929 through 1932. During the same timeframe, the public expressed concern regarding the marital status and state residency of some of the contestants. In fact, according to *Time* magazine, over four hundred women protested the Miss America pageant in 1968. This was also during the period when the women's liberation movement was most active and strong in numbers. Their goal was to assist in freeing women from male supremacy, which included acts of alleged exploitation. The women in attendance at the demonstration threw cosmetics, household cleaning products, and bras into a wastebasket labeled "Freedom Trash Can" and put a crown on a sheep's head. There is also conflicting information about the year that African-Americans could be contestants. Some research states that they began participating in the 1940s. However, stories surrounding Apex state that the first black beauty contestant was Miss Cecilia Cooper, a twenty-three-year-old from New York City. Miss Cooper was a participant in 1953, and the first African-American titleholder was Vanessa Williams in 1984. Nonetheless, this was a proud moment in the history of Madame Sara Spencer Washington's great legacy. Her efforts through the years paved the way for women of color to be able to participate in beauty pageants across America.

As the years continued to progress, major decisions were made about the future of Apex News and Hair Company. In 1956, Holton Hayes announced that Apex News and Hair Company would be investing roughly a quarter of a million dollars in an expansion program, which included creating new products and repackaging current beauty products. Mrs. Hayes believed that the expansion program would result in the strongest increase in sales in Apex's history. Although Apex achieved minimal growth after the venture, the expansion program did not generate the type of sales figures projected. Shortly after the expansion project was underway, one of the most drastic decisions made by Apex News and Hair Company was relocating the organization to Camden, New Jersey. The move prompted layoffs of hundreds of employees who did not transfer to the new location. This was front-page news in Atlantic City's Northside section of the *Atlantic City Free Press* newspaper.

Unfortunately, Apex News and Hair Company's outlook appeared grim as personal issues with some of Apex's key staff members befell. In 1958, Heiress Joan Washington-Hayes divorced Holton Hayes on the grounds of extreme cruelty. In the Mr. and Mrs. section of *Jet Magazine*, it was reported that Joan informed *Jet* that Holton punched her in the nose and mouth in front of friends at a gathering at their home. Holton Hayes received the visitation rights of their three children, and the property they acquired together was divided. "Apex Heiress wins Divorce on Cruelty Charges" (*Jet*, July 31, 1958) The media continued to follow the lives of many key players involved in Madame Sara Spencer Washington's life, including her widow, Shumpert Logan. *Jet* reported that Washington's widow purchased a new home in a new development located in Monroe Park, New Jersey, a suburb of Atlantic City, and was spotted with Philadelphian Hillary Morgan. When questioned by news reporters about their relationship, she denied it being anything but a mutual friendship with Mr. Logan. Her husband, Archie Morgan, a long-term staff member and officer of Apex, separated from his wife. The biggest news about Apex News and Hair Company, only six years after Madame Sara Spencer Washington's passing, was the selling of Apex to Pharmetics Corporation in Baltimore,

Maryland. Pharmetics were the makers of My Knight hairdressing, pomades, and medicinal products. During my conversation with Royston Scott, grandson of Madame Spencer Washington, he mentioned that the company, Pretty Hands and Feet, may have also acquired some portion of Apex. However, I did not find any information about such a business transaction in my research.

In 1960, Joan Washington-Hayes was remarried to Dr. Stanton Scott, head resident surgeon of Provident Hospital in Baltimore, Maryland. Dr. Scott was a graduate of Howard University. The couple was married at the home of Mr. and Mrs. William Gosnell. Joan married again in later years to Walter Earl Walker. I interviewed Madame Sara Spencer Washington's grandson and Joan's son, Royston Scott, over the phone in 2014 while in graduate school writing a paper about Madame Spencer Washington. Royston Scott is the youngest child of Joan and the only offspring after the marriage to Holton Hayes. He inherited many of Madame Sara Spencer Washington's artifacts and memorabilia after his mother's passing. He shared with me that even after the sale of Apex, his mother continued to provide a loving home for their family while, at this point, being employed at a department store in the Baltimore, Maryland area. In our interview, Royston shared that it became rare that anyone in his upbringing conversed about Apex and its history due to the painful ending of Joan's relationship with Holton Hayes. Joan passed on November 7, 2005, at the age of seventy-eight at the Carroll Hospital Center in Westminster. She spent the past few years of her life at Brinton Woods Nursing Home. At the time of her passing, she was survived by her sons Wesley Hayes, Thomas Hayes, and Royston Scott, daughter Savene Hayes, three granddaughters, and a great-grandson.

Royston Scott spoke candidly about his knowledge of his grandmother and the history of Apex. Due to the tumultuous marriage between Holton Hayes and his mother, conversations about the experiences of working at Apex were rare. By the time Royston considered the idea of creating a documentary about "the Madame," as he referred to her in our discussion, his mother had passed, leaving behind photographs, Apex magazines, an oil painting, and other remnants. Royston stated that Sara Spencer Washington did not approve of her courtship with Mr. Hayes and would have objected to his role as Vice-President of Apex. Although Joan was passionate about the company, she wanted to spend more time raising Royston's older siblings and being a homemaker. Joan trusted decisions being made by Holton Hayes and other long-standing board members. Royston stated that his mother was unlucky in love. Royston also shared with me that not only was his father abusive to his mother, but he experienced abuse from him as a child. Royston has not spoken to his father in years. Despite the trauma in Royston's early childhood, he attended college and is a newlywed leading a good life in New York City. Royston is very proud of the accomplishments of his mother and grandmother and is constantly contacted by organizations to learn more about the history of the business since producing his short film. I also learned from speaking with him that there is a bridge in New Jersey that was rebuilt in 1942, and Sara Spencer Washington donated the land.

6

APEX BEAUTY SCHOOLS – THE LONGEST LEGACY

"As long as there are women in the world,
there will be beauty establishments."
—*Sara Spencer Washington*

Years after Apex News and Hair Company was sold, the franchised Apex Beauty Colleges continued to thrive. One of the most successful and long-standing schools was The Apex College of Beauty in Philadelphia, remaining progressive for decades. As of the 1980s, it became the country's oldest black institution of beauty technology. The Apex College of Beauty Culture officially came to Philadelphia in 1928, but advertisements about the schools began in 1921. Although several Apex beauty schools existed throughout the United States, only four were launched by Madame Spencer Washington: one in Atlantic City, two in New York, and one in Philadelphia. Enrollment at the Philadelphia establishment increased at such a speedy pace that in 1935, Sara started looking for a larger location. Madame Spencer Washington sought the assistance of a prominent lawyer named Raymond Pace Alexander to shop around Philadelphia for a building fit for the elite Apex Beauty School. Alexander secured a location on 16th Street and Lombard Street, which he was familiar with because he was involved in acquiring it for the *Philadelphia Tribune*. After $6,900 in improvements, the Lombard Street property was transformed into Apex Beauty School. The Lombard Street location sat right in the heart of an

African-American community and was once used as a nightclub and drug store.

Apex Beauty School opened its doors at its new facility on May 28, 1935, with a grand opening so elaborate that it lasted the entire day. Madame Sara Spencer Washington was known for producing special events filled with African-American celebrities and dignitaries. Like Madame C.J. Walker, she was well-known and respected around the country for her successful business and civic and charitable endeavors. The day-long event concluded with a dedication ceremony at 8:30 PM at which Prince L. Edwoods, advertising manager of the *Philadelphia Tribune*, performed the duty of master of ceremonies, and Rev. John R. Logan, Sr. of St. Simon the Cyrenian Episcopal Church, provided the invocation. A host of prominent figureheads of Philadelphia's African American community gave remarks at the celebration: Major Richard Robert Wright, Sr., (1855–1947), founder of the Georgia State Industrial

College for Colored Youth in Savannah and the Citizens and Southern Bank and Trust Company in Philadelphia; Edward W. Henry (1872–1946), the second African American magistrate appointed in Philadelphia and a United States Congressional candidate in 1932; Dr. John P. Turner (1885–1958), Chief Surgeon at Frederick Douglass Hospital and the first African American to be elected to the Philadelphia School Board; and J. Austin Norris (1893–1976), a local attorney, secretary of the Board of Revision of Taxes, and the founder of the Philadelphia Independent. The involvement of the plethora of distinguished leaders indicated how vital the institution of the Apex Beauty School was to the black community of Philadelphia. Madame Spencer Washington sought to encourage and inspire those who sought a better economic standing during a timeframe in America that offered few opportunities.

Due to the size and amenities of Sara Spencer Washington's Lombard Street location, it became a popular community gathering place for Beauty Culture interests and other miscellaneous community events hosted by various African-American organizations. Apex Hall, the auditorium on the second floor, was sought out for use by a variety of institutions and special interest groups and provided new opportunities for the Apex School to engage more with Beauty Culture and African American communities. Almost immediately after opening the doors of Apex, the State Board of Examiners of Beauty Culture, Apex associations, and alumni groups held meetings in Apex Hall. The auditorium provided a space for dances and dinners, both for Apex groups as well as others. Social events such as movie showings were common for high school children and young adult groups and sometimes drew hundreds of people. Additionally, Apex Beauty College began a routine of hosting open houses where interested students could watch stylists demonstrate techniques taught at the school. Associations such as Delta Sigma Theta sorority and Omega Psi Phi fraternity organized dances in the Hall, and diverse clubs and civic groups such as the Better Business Bureau of the Citizens Civic League, Les Bonne Amis Club, the Selectee Liberty Mothers, and the Fairview Debs Golf Club met in Apex Hall.

Apex College experienced an immediate growth in the number of enrollees at the new building on Lombard Street. In November of 1936, there were eighty-five graduates, and the number of graduates increased by approximately forty percent annually for the next five years. Consequently, the surge in attendees at Apex afforded Madame Spencer Washington to pay off the remaining $6,385 due on the mortgage in December 1936, nearly one year after acquiring the property. By the early 1940s, the school was graduating an average of one hundred students annually and ultimately expanded to two hundred students. The success of Madame Washington's

Philadelphia location, coupled with a widespread interest in African-Americans pursuing a background in Beauty Culture, extended across the eastern portion of the United States, causing Apex to sustain an enrollment of an average of two hundred students for the next decade. In 1944, at least a third of the students enrolled in the school came to Philadelphia from the South, specifically to study at the S. 16th and Lombard Street's Apex location. The attendance at Apex Beauty College grew at a rapid pace, which led to more sophisticated and lengthy commencement ceremonies. The graduation commemorations extended to two days, including divided graduation exercises and baccalaureate sermon. Nationally known African-American leaders came to Philadelphia to participate in the ceremonies. Those involved included: in 1937, Charlotte Hawkins Brown (1883–1961), an author, educator, and founder of the Palmer Memorial Institute in North Carolina; in 1940, Adam Clayton Powell, Jr.

(1908–1972), a civil rights leader and later New York Congressman; in 1941, Mary McLeod Bethune (1875–1950), an educator, philanthropist, and civil rights leader; as well as Armond Wendell Scott (1873–1960), a very popular Washington, DC judge; in 1944, J. Austin Norris (1893–1976), an editor, a civil rights leader, and a lawyer in one of the oldest black law firms in the country (founded with A. Leon Higginbotham); and in 1945, Grant Reynolds (1908–2004), a World War II chaplain, civil rights activist, and a key force in the integration of the United States military.

By 1940, the Apex Beauty School was the leading Beauty Culture school for African Americans in Philadelphia. Ten out of the twenty-seven beauty schools in Philadelphia were for and run by African Americans. Apex was by far the largest. The next largest was likely the Poro School of Beauty Culture, which operated nearby at 629 S. Broad Street. All the other schools were fairly small locally run operations – not part of a larger beauty school chain – managed by African American women in houses and small storefronts throughout the city. These smaller operations graduated between thirty-five and fifty students a year during the 1930s and 40s. The largest among these was the Cartier Beauty School, founded by Ruth Matilda Carter (ca. 1888–1979) in 1933. At its peak in 1946, it had eighty-two graduates, but for the other years reported, the average was around forty.

In 1944, The Apex Beauty School was forced out of its Lombard Street location by the government. The federal government confiscated the building due to a shortage of enough properties for African-Americans during the war. The government wanted the building to set up a venereal disease clinic for the Frederick Douglass Hospital that was just down the street. After failed discussions with the government arranged by Sara's attorney, Raymond Pace Alexander, Madame Washington began quickly looking for another location for her ever-growing Apex Beauty School. Raymond Alexander's brother, Scholley, assisted in finding a new location for Apex Beauty College. Apex Beauty School moved to 521-25 South Broad Street. The school remained at this location until the beauty school closed its doors in 1977 in South Philadelphia, due to a decline in enrollment. The school hurried to find another building by the beginning of June and continue its program for the over one hundred students it had enrolled. To make matters worse, the government was only willing to pay the Apex School $8,500 for the property. Alexander, however, contested the valuation and got the government to pay Mme. Washington $13,500 for the property. In usual Apex fashion, a formal dedication of the new building occurred in June of 1945. Dr. Charlotte Hawkins Brown returned to Philadelphia to be the principal speaker. Tenor Luther Saxon (1916–2017), who had recently appeared in Carmon Jones, and

Camilla Ella Williams (1919–2012), the first African American to receive a regular contract with a major American opera company, was present to sing at the ceremony.

Certainly, the longevity and success of the Philadelphia franchise of Apex Beauty Schools were due to strong leadership. Their success demonstrated that black women were quite capable of owning and running a company in the early to mid-1900s. After several decades, the market became saturated with options to learn beauty techniques. Remaining competitive was a key factor. Also, a succession plan in the event of a change in president more than other executive positions is essential. Nothing is guaranteed, as I learned from Sara's story. Even with a plan, change is inevitable and uncontrollable. What is remarkable about Sara is that she had a vision for Apex, which was huge, bold, and brave. Madame Sara Spencer Washington was a smart and kind but shrewd businesswoman who insisted that people of color be treated with dignity and respect, in any instances in America. The worth of black females in the United States has primarily been appreciated by their own race or outside of the United States. Today, standards of beauty have changed and morphed into a bountiful array of options for hairstyling and hair care. As our history shows, all women have been discriminated against in a variety of ways. Look at Mary Bloomer, for example, who was objected to ridicule by white men for wearing pants, formally known as bloomers. She used her literary voice by starting a newspaper and wrote about women's suffrage. American networks did not televise women wearing pants until The Dick Van Dyke Show. Madame Sara Spencer Washington was instrumental in shaping the definition of African-American beauty in the United States from the 1920s through the 1950s.

Another vital extension of Madame Sara Spencer Washington's royal legacy stems from one of her male students and graduates of her Apex Beauty College, once located in Atlanta,

Georgia. Dr. Nathaniel Bronner Sr. graduated from Apex Beauty College in 1939. Dr. Nathaniel Bronner Sr. (1914-1993) found inspiration strolling down Auburn Street in Atlanta, Georgia, where the biggest African-American beauty giants Madame C.J. Walker, Annie Turnbo-Malone, and Madame Sara Spencer Washington opened beauty colleges. Their colleges were in the Sweet Auburn Historic District, which is about one and a half miles long, between Courtland Street and Interstate 75/85 in downtown Atlanta. The name "Sweet Auburn" was coined by John Wesley Dobbs (1882-1961), civic and political activist, because wealthy businesses were owned and operated by Blacks in this area. He was the only man in his graduating class. Dr. Nathaniel Bronner Sr. founded The Bronner Brothers company and the nation's largest African-American hair show, which is held bi-annually. Dr. Nathaniel Bronner Sr. and his brother, Arthur, founded Bronner Brothers in 1947. The Bronner Brothers

International Beauty Show has been in existence for seventy-two years. The show attracts tens of thousands of hair care experts who participate in hair-style competitions and attend courses on various relevant hairstyles and techniques. Most attendees are black women. It must have seemed odd to witness a man attending a beauty college in the 1930s, but Dr. Nathaniel Bronner was an opportunist who recognized a growing economic trend in the African-American hair care market. Dr. Nathaniel Bronner Sr. was raised in Kelly, Georgia, but fled to Atlanta, Georgia, after the Ku Klux Klan burned down their family home twice. Dr. Bronner enrolled at Morehouse College and secured a paper route to make money. Inspired by the early beauty giants, Dr. Bronner started carrying hair and beauty products from his sister's salon along with him while delivering newspapers. He enrolled in Apex Beauty College and proceeded to build his own empire, achieving millionaire status, which has been carried on by the men in the Bronner family. Madame Spencer Washington's influence and inspiration live through the Bronner family business.

Pictured here is the Apex Beauty College, Class of 1950. Location is unknown but possibly taken in Atlantic City, New Jersey. (Alfred M. Heston Collection, Atlantic City Free Public Library.)

Pictured here is another graduating class from Apex Beauty College. Although few in numbers, men attended Apex. Included in the photograph is one male graduate, in the center of the last row. (Alfred M. Heston Collection, Atlantic City Free Public Library.)

Pictured here is Apex Beauty College's Class of 1952. Location is most likely in Atlantic City, New Jersey. (Alfred M. Heston Collection, Atlantic City Free Public Library.)

CONCLUSION

Today, a historical marker in honor of Madame Spencer Washington is located on the Southwest Corner of North Martin Luther King, Jr. Boulevard and Arctic Avenue in Atlantic City in the neighborhood where Apex News and Hair existed. There are also several buildings in New Jersey, New York, and Pennsylvania once owned by Madame Sara Spencer Washington that were utilized by other businesses. In 1997, Sara was inducted into the Atlantic County Women's Hall of Fame. "The Madame" also received an honorary doctoral degree from Northwestern University and given her own day of recognition in Atlantic City in the form of a resolution (89), dated February 23, 2019. In 2016, Sara Spencer Washington's grandson Royston Scott released an award-winning short-story film documentary about his grandmother. The showing of the documentary has prompted other organizations and institutions to inquire about Sara's history, other pieces of information, and artifacts to be shared by others. Since the raised awareness of Madame Washington's accomplishments, a Sara Spencer Washington exhibit once displayed inside of the Atlantic City Free Public Library has been relocated to Boardwalk Hall in Atlantic City, where more visitors can see her artifacts.

There's still a lot about the history of Apex that may never be discovered or may take some time to uncover, because of the move from New Jersey to Maryland. Enough of Sara's history remains intact to teach readers about what one determined woman was able to achieve and what it took to accomplish it. Sara's footprint has been a trail that has been worth following because of the milestones she achieved in the early to mid-1900s in America and internationally. My final task over the project of researching Madame Washington was to locate any remains of her legacy that could be preserved. An Atlantic City native told me that there was one remaining Apex building. I decided to do something to preserve the location. I contacted the New Jersey Preservation office and filed paperwork that will make it impossible for the Apex building to be destroyed. Hopefully, this narrative will add to the evidence to support their decision.

As I've discussed Madame Washington's history with people I meet, I am often asked why no one has ever heard about her. This is a question that I hope to be asked about much of the literary work I do. I am grateful that while researching a different topic, I stumbled across Sara, and my inquisitiveness led me to research the exceptional path she led. Decades later, her story is relevant to topics in our society today, such as racism, sexism, self-image issues, and gender equality. Sara's template to become an international businesswoman can be examined and duplicated by Generation X, Y, or Z.

As I work on this close, Sara's story broadens into Hair Expos, the Smithsonian, and a scholarship is awarded to a student interested in Chemistry at Stockton University. I hope that this Golden Beauty Boss' story will continue to reach the masses and inspire others, especially women entrepreneurs and leaders, to fulfill their dreams fearlessly. There are little girls, women, and grandmothers with the fire of Sara in them. May it be lit with a golden light of vision.

SELECTED BIBLIOGRAPHY

"A. Norris Addresses Apex Graduates," *Philadelphia Tribune*, June 17, 1944.

Apex Country Club Photograph Collection (H038). Atlantic City Free Public Library, Atlantic City, New Jersey. April 2015.

"Apex Announces 63rd commencement." *New York Amsterdam News*. June 6, 1981, 24.

"Apex Alumni Gives Memorial Luncheon." *Philadelphia Tribune*, March 25, 1958, 7.

"Apex Beauty College Graduates Well Trained Beauticians," *Philadelphia Tribune*, November 19, 1936.

"Apex Company Hires Two Alert Young Men." *Philadelphia Tribune*. January 5, 1954, 12.

"Apex Company Wins $13,500 Suit, Granted Sum for Building Seizure," *Philadelphia Tribune*, November 4, 1944.

"Apex School Forced to Close Shop." Philadelphia Tribune. October 18, 1977, 27.

"Apex Float Will Be in AC Parade." *New York Amsterdam News*. August 20 5th 1956, 9.

"Apex Founder Will Probate Set Tuesday." *Baltimore Afro-American.*, April 7, 1953.

"Apex Grad Returns to Africa." *Philadelphia Tribune.*, February 23, 1954, 5.

"Apex Graduates to Hear Mary McLeod Bethune," *Philadelphia Tribune*, June 5, 1941.

"Apex Graduates Record Classes." *New York Amsterdam News.*, July 2, 1955, 12.

"Apex Head Donates Funds to Hospital." *Philadelphia Tribune.* January 5, 1954, 6.

"Apex Holds Open House for Public." *Philadelphia Tribune.*

"Apex Makes Beauty Market News with Liquid Press." *New York Amsterdam News.* August 7, 1954, 10.

"Apex Meeting." *New York Amsterdam News.* May 1, 1965, 11.

"Apex Opens School at New Site: Building Equipped with Latest Inventions for Beauty Culture." *Philadelphia Tribune*, May 30, 1935.

"Apex President Injured in Virginia." *Philadelphia Tribune*, March 3, 1938, 3. Print.

"Apex Schools Monument to Famed Woman. *New York Amsterdam News.* Feb. 12, 1949, 7.

"Apex School Lists 24th Graduation," *Philadelphia Tribune*, June 5, 1955.

"Appointed Supervisor in Apex Schools." *Philadelphia Tribune*, 8.

"Atlanta Honors APEX President." *Philadelphia Tribune* May 15, 1941.

Atlantic City Board of Trade. Board of Trade: Annual Directory. Atlantic City, NJ: The Board, various years. Atlantic City Free Public Library, Atlantic City, New Jersey. April 2015.

"Banquet Planned by Apex Alumni." Philadelphia Tribune March 27, 1979, 19.

Barner, George. Harlem Girl in the Miss America Beauty Pageant. *New York Amsterdam News*; September 12, 1959, 1.

"Beauticians Gather at Fellowship Tea." *Philadelphia Tribune.*, April 14, 1953, 6.

"Beauty Culture Schools," Pennsylvania Public Education Bulletin 7, no. 6 (February 1940), 18–19.

Clairborne, Carl C. "Madame Washington: A Study in Race Prejudice."

Commire, Anne and Klezmer, Deborah. "Dictionary of Women Worldwide: 25,000 Women Through the Ages. Detroit: Yorkin Publications, 2007. 1967. Gale Virtual Reference Library. Web. 9 Feb. 2015.

Compian, Felicia. Successful professionals look bad to their family's deep roots in AC. Hometown *Atlantic City Free Press*. March 16, 2011.

Cunningham, Evelyn. "Apex is Outmoding Primitive Labels: Straighten, Pressing, Beautician." *Pittsburgh Courier*, August 8, 1959, C3.

"Daughter Gets 51% Stock in Apex Co." *Baltimore Afro-American.* March 31, 1953.

"Daughter Willed Apex Company Control." *Philadelphia Tribune.*, April 4, 1953, 1.

Driskell, Jay. "Making waves: Beauty Salons and the Black Freedom Struggle." http://americanhistory.si.edu/blog/making-waves-beauty-salons-and-black-freedom-struggle. Oct. 26, 2018. Web.

Employment Drive by Apex: Famous Concern Marks July as Progress Month for Firm. *New York Amsterdam News*. July 6, 1940, 23.

Goddard, Richlyn F. *Three Months to Hurry and Nine Months to Worry: Resort life for African Americans in Atlantic City, NJ* 1850-1940. Ph.D. dissertation. Washington, DC: Howard University, 2001.

"Graduates Receive Diplomas," *Philadelphia Tribune*, October 20, 1932.

"Hair Co. Devising New Products, New Methods." *Pittsburgh Courier*. January 29, 1955, 17.

History. www.pomonagolfcourse.com/history November 29, 2017. Web.

Histrionic Pageant Honors Apex Head. *Philadelphia Tribune*. Feb 17, 1953, 7.

Jasper, John. "Would She have Lived Longer?" *The Baltimore Afro-Americas*, April 7, 1953.

John-Ferguson, Ruth. The Historical Society of Pennsylvania. Collection 3075, Ruth John Ferguson Papers 1901-1985. The Historical Society of Pennsylvania. November 2018.

Johnson, Nelson. *The Northside: African Americans and the Creation of Atlantic City.* New Jersey: Plexus Publishing, Inc., 2010.

"Minister Declares Race Is Badly Miseducated," *Philadelphia Tribune*, July 4, 1940.

"Mid-Term Apex Beauty College Graduating Class,"
Philadelphia Tribune, August 13, 1941.

McKlelvey, Wallace. Two South Jersey Legends Up for
Inclusion in this Year's New Jersey Hall of Fame.
Tribune Business News. The Press of Atlantic City.
2013. Internet.

"Moving Pictures Shown in Apex School's 'At
Home'," *Philadelphia Tribune*, 9 May 1940.

"Mother of Apex Beauty School's Owner is Dead."
Philadelphia Tribune. December 30, 1969, 3.

"Mrs. J.W. Hayes Heads Apex News, Hair Co." *The
Pittsburgh Courier*. March 15, 1956, 6.

"No Substitute for Hard Work Speaker Tells Apex
Graduates," *Philadelphia Tribune*, July 7, 1938.

Negroes Still Own Apex Co., *Philadelphia Tribune*,
August 18, 1956, 1.

"News and Analyst of the website digital Harlem:
everyday life, 1950 through 1930.

Nigerian Graduates from Apex, *New York Amsterdam
News*, Oct. 20, 1962, 14.

"106 Diplomas to Apex Grads This Week:
Baccalaureate Sermon Held for First Time by
Local School," Philadelphia Tribune, June 19,
1941.

"1,000 Apex Student Beauty Schools Located in 9
Cities; Company Lost $46,000 in Closed Banks;
Graduates Throughout the Country Total
20,000; Twenty-Pass Pennsylvania Board," Afro-
American, 29 June 1935.

Palmer, Colin A., Encyclopedia of African-American Culture and History, volume to 2nd edition Detroit: McMillan reference USA 2006, 753.

Peterson, Robert A. *Patriots, Pirates, and Pineys: 60 Who Shaped New Jersey* pp. 133-134; Plexus Publishing, Inc. Medford, New Jersey. 1998.

"Philadelphia. Apex Agents Meet," *Philadelphia Tribune*, August 8, 1935.

"Phila's Leading Businesses Welcome Apex, Plaque to Be Unveiled at Open House Ceremony," *Philadelphia Tribune*, June 30, 1935.

Sara Spencer Washington and Apex Photographs. Charles L Blockson Afro-American Collection. Temple University, Philadelphia, PA. 2017.

Sarah Spencer Washington's Mother Dead: Was Ill 3 days Atlantic City. *Philadelphia Tribune.* July 1, 1937, 20.

SD Walker Inc versus Brigantine Beach Hotel Corporation, New Jersey Superior Court March 1, 1957, http://law.justia.com/cases/new-jersey /appellatte-division-published/1957/44-n-j-super-193... Web. 2/23/2015.

"State Beauty Culture Board to Meet Here," *Philadelphia Tribune*, July 11, 1935.

Summers, Gerrie. Four Pioneering Black Cosmetics. http://multiculturalbeauty.about.com/od/Black /a/Black-Cosmetics-Pioneers.htm. 2/2/2015.

The Bantu World. [Johannesburg South Africa: Bantu World Ltd] 2014. Web.

"The 1937 Graduating Class of The Apex Beauty College in Philadelphia," *Philadelphia Tribune*, November 18, 1937.

The Sara Spencer Washington Story. Scott, Royston. 2016. Film Documentary.

Walker, Joan. "Joan Sarah Walker died." *The Gazette*. November 17, 2005.

Waltzer, Jim. "The Beauty Beating the Odds." *Atlantic City Weekly.* October 20, 2005.

Washington, Sara S., "Beauty Products and Their Use." The Apex News and Hair Company, Atlantic City Free Public Library, Atlantic City, New Jersey. April 2015.

Washington, Sara S., Local History Subject File – Black Businesses, Atlantic City Free Public Library, Atlantic City, New Jersey. April 2015.

Washington, Sara S., Local History Biography File – Sarah Spencer Washington. Atlantic City Free Public Library, Atlantic City, New Jersey. April 2015.

Washington, Sara S., Sarah Spencer Washington Exhibit Materials (HEx001). Atlantic City Free Public Library, Atlantic City, New Jersey April 2015.

Washington, Sara S., Apex Country Club Photograph Collection (H038). Atlantic City Free Public Library, Atlantic City, New Jersey April 2015.

Weinbaum, Alvis Eve... (and others), editor. "The Modern Girl Around the World." Duke University Press, 2008.

Weisbrot, Robert. "Father Divine." Encyclopedia of Religion. Ed. Lindsay Jones. 2nd ed. Vol. 5. Detroit: Macmillan Reference USA, 2005. 3006-3007. Gale Virtual Reference Library. Web. 3 Mar. 2015.

"Woman Heads Big Business Hires Many." *Philadelphia Tribune*, Oct. 6, 1932, 5.

ABOUT THE AUTHOR

After curating an exhibit of photos from photographer, John W. Mosley for her thesis project, Cheryl Woodruff-Brooks completed her first book, *Chicken Bone Beach: A Pictorial History of Atlantic City's Missouri Avenue Beach* (Sunbury Press) in 2017, which was nominated for a 2017 Literary Award with the Schomburg Center in New York City, used

in classrooms at Purdue University and refer-
enced in The Oxford Handbook of American
Folklore and Folklife Studies. Cheryl has been
involved in speaking engagements discussing
Chicken Bone Beach, including an event
called, Black Girl Beach Day which took
place on the sands of historical Chicken Bone
Beach, Rowan University, and the Atlantic
City Historical Museum. Cheryl has been
interviewed by several newspapers such as
the *Philadelphia Tribune*, celebrity strategist
and on-air radio personality Dyana Williams
of Philadelphia's Radio One, IHeart Radio,
podcasts, and online radio stations. Cheryl
is also a professional singer/songwriter,
writing songs for her own music projects and
for other artists.

Made in the USA
Middletown, DE
30 June 2020